st★r
DROP

ISBN 978-0-9681025-7-2

PRINTED IN CANADA

I BOX
Publishing

PROLOGUE

IN ADVENTURE STORIES, THERE'S ALWAYS A SOFT SPOT TO LAND AND *NOBODY* HAS TO PEE.

≡SIGH≡

CHAPTER ONE

"INTO THE UNKNOWN"

¿AHEM?

EXCUSE ME...

I'M NEW HERE.

I LOST ALL MY **MONEY** AND MY **LUGGAGE**, AND I WAS WONDERING IF MAYBE YOU HAD ANY <u>ADVICE</u>.

NO, NO...

I CAN'T SAY THAT.

GOTTA COME UP WITH SOME-THING <u>GOOD</u>.

...

8

ARE YOU SURE ABOUT THIS?

ABSOLUTELY!

SLEEPING ON THE COUCH IS A TIME-HONORED TRADITION.

EVERYBODY FINDS THEM-SELVES DOWN AND OUT AT LEAST ONCE IN THEIR LIFE.

I'M JUST GLAD I CAN HELP.

YOU CAN STAY HERE AS LONG AS YOU NEED.

-YOU'RE MY GUEST!

GOSH.

I DON'T KNOW WHAT TO SAY.

THANK-YOU SO MUCH!

I'LL START LOOKING FOR WORK RIGHT AWAY.

COME ON. I'LL BUY YOU LUNCH.

I WANT TO HEAR ALL ABOUT YOU.

34

MY FATHER WOULD HAVE SENT ME WITH A HALF MILLION **UG-TROOPS** AND A FLOATING **BATTLE PALACE**.

HE WOULD HAVE DEMANDED TRIBUTES FROM THE NATIVE POPULACE.

TOTAL PLANETARY DOMINATION!

BUT I DIDN'T WANT THAT!

I THINK THAT'S HORRIBLE.

YOU'RE ACTUALLY QUITE LUCKY, YOU KNOW. - MY BROTHER ALMOST GOT THIS PLANET.

YOUR BROTHER?

CAREGA.

I DON'T REALLY WANT TO TALK ABOUT HIM.

HMPH.

I JUST WANTED TO COME BY MYSELF AND MAKE FRIENDS AND GET AWAY FROM THE EMPIRE.

THIS IS DEPRESSING.

JEN JACOBS, PLEASE DON'T TREAT ME ANY DIFFERENTLY!

I REALLY WANT TO BE YOUR FRIEND!

MAYBE I SHOULDN'T HAVE TOLD YOU ABOUT ME, BUT REAL FRIENDSHIPS CAN'T WORK UNLESS PEOPLE ARE **HONEST** AND **OPEN**.

MY MOM WARNED ME ABOUT LIVING WITH ROOM MATES.

AM I MESSING THIS UP?

OKAY. FIRST THINGS FIRST.

YOU WANT TO FIT IN AROUND HERE?

YES.

CAN YOU HELP ME?

LUNCH SPECIAL

I CAN TRY.

TO START WITH, IS THAT ALL YOU HAVE TO WEAR?

YES.

IT'S NOT APPROPRIATE, IS IT?

SO WHERE ARE WE OFF TO TODAY?

I'M GOING SHOPPING FOR SOME MORE SUITABLE GARMENTS.

—I REALIZE THAT IT LOOKS AS THOUGH I'M FROM OFF-WORLD, BUT REALLY I JUST HAVE POOR TASTE IN ATTIRE.

—MY FRIEND, JEN IS HELPING ME.

I SEE.

GOOD LUCK WITH THAT.

THANK-YOU!

WOW!

YOU CAN SEE MUCH MORE OF HUMAN CULTURE FROM A BUS THAN YOU CAN FROM A BOXCAR.

YOU HAVE SUCH PRETTY BUILDINGS!

—AND I'VE NEVER SEEN SO MANY PERSONAL TRANSPORTS USING WHEELS INSTEAD OF PULSE-PLATES.

THEY'RE SO CUTE!

THEY MUST BE VERY SATISFYING TO PILOT, ROLLING RIGHT ON THE VERY GROUND LIKE THAT!

I NEVER REALLY CONSIDERED IT BEFORE.

OH, JEN!

I AM VERY EXCITED ABOUT THIS TRIP!

I CAN SEE THAT.

CHAPTER TWO

"ACCLIMATIZATION"

WELL, HERE WE ARE AT THE MALL.

THE MALL...

THESE LITTLE SHOPS EACH SELL SOMETHING DIFFERENT. —WE'RE LOOKING FOR WOMEN'S CLOTHES.

THIS PLACE IS LIKE AN IMPERIAL SYSTEM FORTRESS, BUT WITH MORE COLOR AND LESS WEAPONRY.

DO PEOPLE COME HERE OF THEIR OWN FREE WILL?

SURE. WHAT DO YOU MEAN?

I DON'T KNOW... THERE'S SOMETHING VERY WEIRD ABOUT THIS PLACE. —WHAT'S THAT NOISE?

ARE THERE SUB-SENSORIES BEING BROADCAST?

AND WHY IS THE LIGHT FLICKERING?

THE LIGHT IS FLICKERING!

YEAH. —JUST ON THE EDGE OF MY PERCEPTION.

THIS PLACE FEELS ALL WRONG.

GEE. I DON'T KNOW WHAT YOU MEAN.

HM... ACTUALLY, THIS IS A LOT LIKE AN IMPERIAL SYSTEM FORTRESS!

DO YOU STILL WANT TO STAY AND LOOK FOR CLOTHES?

SURE. WHY NOT?

I'M USED TO THIS KIND OF ENVIRONMENT. —IT'S JUST STRANGE TO FIND IT HERE ON EARTH.

IT'S ALMOST AS THOUGH...

COME ON. —I LOVE THIS SHOP!

HM... YOU HAVE EXPENSIVE TASTE...

WHEN I FIND MY MEANS OF EMPLOYMENT, I'LL BE SURE TO COMPENSATE YOU FULLY.

YEAH... —BUT I DON'T HAVE MUCH MONEY RIGHT **NOW**.

—AND YOU'LL NEED MORE THAN JUST ONE OUTFIT...

I DIDN'T REALLY THINK ABOUT THIS...

OH. —WILL I NOT BE ABLE TO GET PROPER ATTIRE AFTER ALL..?

I'M REALLY SORRY, ASHELLE.

THAT'S OKAY.

I'LL SIMPLY RESIGN MYSELF TO NOT FITTING IN. —IT WILL BE MY **LOT IN LIFE.**

HOW TRAGIC.

EXCUSE ME. —I'M SORRY FOR LISTENING IN, BUT YOU KNOW THERE **ARE** PLACES WHERE CLOTHES COST ALMOST NO MONEY..?

MY **JUMP-SUIT** COST NO MONEY, BUT I HAD TO JOIN THE MILITARY FIRST.

NO, NO, —IT'S NOT THE ARMY. —IT'S GOOD, NORMAL CLOTHES, BUT JUST VERY INEXPENSIVE.

REALLY? WHERE?

LATER...

ARE WE NEAR THE 'DISCOUNT STORE' YET..?

I DON'T KNOW. SHE SAID IT WAS FIFTEEN MINUTES ALONG THIS ROAD, BUT I'M BEGINNING TO THINK SHE ASSUMED WE HAD A <u>CAR</u>...

HM... IT SEEMS ODD THAT WE SHOULD HAVE TO WALK WHEN THERE ARE SO MANY **TRANSPORTS** IN USE.

MANY OF THEM HAVE ONLY **ONE** PERSON INSIDE... —MAYBE SOMEBODY WILL LET US TRAVEL WITH THEM...

I SAID **NO,** ALREADY!

YOU'RE NUTS!

COME ON! IT'S EASY.

I'LL SHOW YOU.

UGH. I'M NOT COMFORTABLE WITH THIS!

JUST BE FIRM, AND COURTEOUS AT THE SAME TIME.

KNOCK KNOCK

HELLO?

HELLO! MY NAME IS **ASHELLE**, AND THIS IS MY FRIEND, **JEN**.

WOULD YOU PLEASE TAKE US TO THE DISCOUNT STORE IN YOUR **PERSONAL TRANSPORT**?

—IT'S BECAUSE I HAVE POOR TASTE IN ATTIRE.

PARDON ME..?

I'M REALLY SORRY ABOUT THIS. —MY FRIEND ISN'T FROM HERE.

SHE'S AN INTERNATIONAL STUDENT FROM FAR AWAY.

SHE DOESN'T KNOW HOW TO ASK FOR THINGS PROPERLY IN OUR CULTURE, BUT SHE'S REALLY VERY NICE.

SHE SOMEHOW GOT THE IDEA THAT YOU COULD JUST KNOCK ON PEOPLE'S DOORS AND ASK FOR THINGS.

I DIDN'T MEAN TO BE UPSETTING.

SHE'S TAKING ME TO THE GLASS-BLOWING WORKSHOP ON THURSDAY!

WILL YOU HELP ME TO REMEMBER?

-I HAVEN'T LEARNED THE DAY NAMES FOR THIS PLANET YET.

UGH!

WHERE ARE YOU GOING?

I HAVE TO STUDY FOR CLASS TOMORROW.

I DON'T HAVE TIME TO BE RUNNING ALL OVER THE PLACE ON CRAZY ADVENTURES!

WHAT? AREN'T YOU GLAD WE WENT?

I GUESS. YEAH...

-I'M JUST TIRED, IS ALL.

YEAH... ME TOO.

I DIDN'T REALLY SLEEP ALL LAST NIGHT ON THE BOX CAR...

OHHH... GOSH.

YOU MUST BE EVEN MORE SLEEPY THAN ME...

COME ON. -LET ME GET YOU SOME BLANKETS.

THANK YOU.

-SIGH-

ZZZ ♥

CHAPTER THREE

"DISTANT DRUMS"

UGH!

BE QUIET, CHARLEN!

YOU DESERVE YOUR PROBLEMS!

I JUST DON'T WANT A BUNCH OF ARMED GOONS SMASHING UP JEN'S HOUSE, AND MAYBE HURTING HER.

YES! IF YOU CARE ABOUT YOUR FRIEND, YOU'LL SUBMIT!

NO! I WON'T GET HURT! WE CAN CALL THE POLICE!

THE POLICE WILL PUT THEM ALL IN JAIL!

HA! THIS WHOLE SETTLEMENT WOULD BE A SMOKING CRATER FIRST!

THEY HAVE TWO BATTLE CRUISERS IN ORBIT.

I DON'T WANT TO INVOLVE THIS PLANET'S AUTHORITIES.

THINGS WOULD GET TOO WEIRD AND COMPLICATED.

OKAY! I'M COMING OUT!

DON'T SHOOT!

BYE, JEN! I'LL BE OKAY!

IT WAS VERY NICE MEETING YOU!

-THANKS FOR LETTING ME SLEEP ON YOUR COUCH!

COME ON!

SIGH.

CHAPTER FOUR

"THE SECOND COMING"

Hi, Mom.
It's Jen.
University is going okay, but I miss you and Dad.

There are so many students here and I've met some nice people, but I have to admit I've been finding it a bit lonely.

I did meet a boy. His name is Tom. We're not together or anything, but he's nice, though I don't really understand him. I guess he's my best friend.

It seems sad to think that somebody who you don't really understand is your best friend. . .

There *was* this one girl I met. . .

She was really cool, and nice and lots of fun to be around.

We were going to be room mates. . .

The only problem was that she thought she was a space alien.

— ASSIGNMENTS ARE DUE ON TUESDAY...

PSST! JEN!

GAH! ASHELLE!? IT'S YOU!

I'M ON THE RUN AGAIN. —I CAME TO FIND YOU.

COME ON. WE CAN'T TALK OUT HERE IN THE OPEN.

WHAT HAPPENED?! ARE YOU OKAY?! HOW DID YOU GET AWAY?

ACTUALLY, THE REVOLUTIONARIES MADE ME THEIR LEADER.

WHAT? I THOUGHT THEY TOOK YOU HOSTAGE.

THEY DID.

BUT I GUESS THEY REALIZED MY VALUE AS A MILITARY TACTICIAN.

I KNOW A LOT OF THE EMPIRE'S SECRETS.

I'VE BEEN INSIDE THE PALACES OF MOST OF MY FATHER'S FRIENDS.

—I'M ACTUALLY SUPPOSED TO BE AT WAR WITH HIM RIGHT NOW.

AT WAR WITH YOUR FATHER?

YES.

IT'S VERY UGLY.

—DIRECTING BATTLE FLEETS AGAINST YOUR DAD...

GOSH.

ACTUALLY, IT TURNS OUT I'M QUITE GOOD AT IT.

—I'VE ALREADY DRIVEN HIS FORCES FROM NEARLY TWO HUNDRED WORLDS.

THE REVOLUTIONISTS KEEP PROMOTING ME.

I THINK I'M A GENERAL OR AN ADMIRAL OR SOMETHING...

SO WHAT ARE YOU DOING BACK HERE?

WELL, EVEN THOUGH I DON'T LIKE THE EMPIRE, I DISLIKE FIGHTING EVEN MORE.

AND I FELT BAD FOR MY FATHER.

SO NOW THE REVOLUTION WANTS ME BACK, AND THE EMPIRE WANTS MY <u>HEAD</u>.

CAN I HIDE IN YOUR HOUSE AGAIN?

WELL, HERE WE ARE.

HOME AGAIN.

THEY'RE REPAIRING YOUR HOUSE FROM THE BLASTER BATTLE WHEN I WAS TAKEN HOSTAGE.

YEAH. THEY HAVE TO PUT UP NEW SIDING.

THE LAND-LADY WAS REALLY UPSET.

GOSH. I'M SORRY TO HEAR THAT.

I GOT NERVOUS WHEN SHE ASKED ME WHAT HAPPENED.

I TOLD HER IT WAS SOME KIDS USING FIREWORKS.

I DIDN'T KNOW WHAT ELSE TO SAY.

-I FEEL BAD ABOUT LYING, BUT THE TRUTH IS JUST TOO WEIRD.

I NEED TO GET BACK TO MY LANDING POD!

PRINCESS!

WHENEVER I MAKE TEA FOR PEOPLE, IT ALWAYS ENDS UP GOING COLD.

OKAY. WHERE DID I HIDE MY DROP POD?

PRINCESS!

YOU MUST NOT LEAVE THIS PLANET!

IT IS NOT SAFE!

WELL, I DON'T HAVE MUCH CHOICE, DO I?

—I NEED TO WARN MY FRIENDS IN THE FLEET ABOUT YOUR HORRIBLE TEMPORAL BEAM SHIPS!

THEY ARE NOT MINE...

WHAT ARE YOU DOING?

I'M BUILDING A DIMENSIONAL LOOP TRANS- MITTER!

SSS

IS THAT MY LAP-TOP?

EVEN THOUGH I AM STRANDED MILLIONS OF LIGHT- YEARS FROM MY PEOPLE, I MUST STILL ATTEMPT CONTACT!

I HAVE DISCOVERED THAT THE EMPIRE PLANS TO USE A HORRIFYING NEW SECRET WEAPON TO LAY WASTE TO THE REVOLUTIONARY FLEET!

MY COMPATRIOTS MUST BE ALERTED TO THE DANGER!

THE EMPIRE'S NEW TEMPORAL WEAPON SHATTERS TIME AND SPACE LIKE GLASS, BUT IF WE ARE CLEVER AND RESOURCEFUL, WE CAN STILL DEFEAT THEM.

—WE HAVE TWO TYPE-J CRUISERS WITH GRAVITY INFLUX REACTORS.

—THAT'S OUR CHANCE!

GRAVITY— WHAT REACTORS?

IT'S AN OUT- MODED STAR VOYAGE TECHNOLOGY.

THEY'RE OLD AND SLOW, BUT THEY CAN CREATE AN INTERFERENCE ZONE IN WHICH TEMPORAL TECH- NOLOGY GETS MUDDLED.

THE EMPIRE'S NEW WEAPON CAN BE RENDERED USELESS!

THAT DOES SOUND CLEVER.

CHAPTER FIVE

"EMPLOYMENT"

HELLO? YES, SHE'S HERE. -JUST A MOMENT.

IS IT THE STOVEHOUSE PUB CALLING TO SAY IF THEY WANT TO HIRE ME?

YES? UH-HUH. ... OH.

YES, I UNDERSTAND. THANK-YOU. GOODBYE.

CLICK

YOU DIDN'T GET THE JOB?

THEY SAID THEY LIKED ME, BUT THAT ALL THE OTHER APPLICANTS HAD EXPERIENCE IN WAITRESSING.

OH, ASHELLE. I'M SORRY.

BAH! THIS IS AWFUL!

HOW CAN I GAIN JOB EXPERIENCE IF NOBODY WILL HIRE ME BECAUSE I DON'T HAVE JOB EXPERIENCE?

IT'S A PARADOX!

OR DO YOU THINK MAYBE THEY JUST DIDN'T LIKE ME?

-WHAT IF THEY FOUND ME UN-LIKABLE BUT WERE TOO POLITE TO SAY SO?

ARGH! I'M A PRINCESS!

-MY NAME IS RESPECTED ACROSS TWO THOUSAND WORLDS IN THE GALACTIC IMPERIUM, BUT I CAN'T EVEN GET A JOB AT THE STOVE-HOUSE PUB. THE ONLY PLACE I'VE EVER REALLY WANTED TO WORK!

OH, THE IRONY IS THICK AND DREADFUL!

YOUR WORLD IS CLOSED TO ME! -I'LL NEVER FIT IN!

YOU'RE BLOWING THIS OUT OF PROPORTION. IT'S NOT THAT BAD.

I DIDN'T GET THE FIRST JOB I APPLIED FOR EITHER.

-IT JUST TAKES A FEW TRIES AND A BIT OF LUCK.

REALLY?

EVEN YOU WERE CRUELLY SPURNED ON YOUR FIRST ATTEMPT?

THE BANK MANAGER?

I DON'T KNOW. —YOU'RE THE ONE WHO WORKS HERE.

JUST A MOMENT. I'LL GO GET HER.

THANK-YOU!

♪

CAN I HELP YOU?

YES! I AM SEEKING EMPLOYMENT.

—I AM VERY GOOD AT *TACTICAL DATA ANALYSIS*.

EVEN THOUGH I HAVE NO DIRECT TRAINING IN FINANCES, I AM CONFIDENT MY SKILLS WILL BE A BENEFIT TO YOUR TEAM!

HOW DID IT GO?

THEY GAVE ME THIS DOCUMENT AND TOLD ME TO FILL IT OUT.

A JOB APPLICATION FORM.

"EDUCATION.."? HM...

WELL I RAN AWAY FROM THE *IMPERIAL MILITARY ACADAMY* BEFORE GRADUATING.

—I HAD TO BLOW UP THE STARPORT SO NOBODY COULD CHASE ME.

MAYBE YOU SHOULDN'T MENTION THAT.

"PREVIOUS EMPLOYERS"?

THE *GALACTIC REVOLUTIONARY FORCES* DON'T HAVE A DAY-TIME CONTACT NUMBER!

WELL I **SAID** A BANK JOB PROBABLY WASN'T FOR YOU.

UGH! I HAVE NO REFERENCES! MY LIFE IS TOO **WEIRD!**

—I'M TWENTY-ONE, AND ALL I HAVE TO SHOW FOR IT IS A TRAIL OF **BROKEN ALLIANCES** AND **UPSET MILITARIES!!**

NOW I CAN'T GET A **JOB!**

—IF ONLY I HAD A CHANCE, I'D SHOW WHAT A GOOD EMPLOYEE I COULD BE!

I'D EARN DIGNITY AND RESPECT!

BUT INSTEAD I DON'T HAVE A SINGLE REFERENCE. **ALL OF CIVILIZATION HATES ME!**

WHAT? —NOW THAT'S JUST SILLY!

;SNIFF; IT'S TRUE.

THE EMPIRE WANTS TO HANG ME FOR **TREASON.** —AND I ABANDONED THE **GALACTIC REVOLUTIONARY** FORCES IN THEIR TIME OF DIRE NEED.

—I'VE PROVEN UNTRUSTWORTHY TO **EVERYBODY.**

I CAN'T THINK OF A **SINGLE** PERSON I COULD ASK FOR A JOB RECOMMENDATION.

—BUT I **CAN** THINK OF **TWO** WHOLE SIDES IN AN INTER-GALACTIC WAR THAT WOULD TELL PEOPLE **NOT** TO HIRE ME.

THERE ARE NOW ENTIRE STAR SYSTEMS WHERE I WOULD BE EITHER SPAT ON...

—OR ARRESTED ON SIGHT!

—THAT'S LIKE FIVE HUNDRED BILLION PEOPLE!

ASHELLE! GOOD NEWS!

-I MIGHT HAVE FOUND YOU A JOB!

REALLY?

TOM HAS A FRIEND WHOSE UNCLE RUNS A BED AND BREAKFAST IN THE AREA.

A BED AND BREAKFAST?

IT'S LIKE A SMALL HOTEL INSIDE A PRETTY HOUSE.

ALL THE GUESTS EAT BREAKFAST TOGETHER. IT'S LIKE VISITING A NICE FAMILY'S HOME.

WOW!

COME ON. -LET'S GET YOU INTO THAT INTERVIEW OUTFIT.

HI, GUYS! THIS IS MY FRIEND, DAVE.

DAVE, THIS IS ASHELLE.

PLEASED TO MEET YOU!

ARE YOU SURE ABOUT THIS?

IT'S OKAY! —SHE JUST NEEDS A CHANCE FOR PEOPLE TO LIKE HER!

I LEARNED HOW TO BE CALM IN THE FACE OF **DIRE** COMBAT, SO IMPRESSING YOUR UNCLE SHOULD BE EASY!

I'M MORE WORRIED ABOUT LASER-GUN BATTLES AT THE B&B.

HEY UNCLE GEORGE, —THIS IS THE GIRL I WAS TELLING YOU ABOUT

'ASHELLE' IS IT?

PLEASED TO MEET YOU!

I'M PLEASED TO MEET YOU, TOO!

WHY DON'T THE REST OF YOU GO MAKE SOMETHING TO EAT WHILE I INTERVIEW ASHELLE?

THIS WAY GUYS!

SO ASHELLE... -TELL ME ABOUT YOURSELF.

WELL, I'M A HARD WORKER.

-AND I LIKE HELPING PEOPLE. -JEN TAUGHT ME HOW TO SCRUB DISHES AND PUT TOWELS IN THE WASHING MACHINE.

JEN HAD TO TEACH YOU HOW TO WASH DISHES?

-IN MY HOME WE HAD SERVANTS, BUT JEN SAYS I HAVE A KNACK FOR IT.

I SEE... AND HOW ARE YOU AT COOKING?

I LEARNED HOW TO MAKE FRIED EGGS AND TOAST.

IT'S VERY TASTY.

FRIED EGGS, HUH?

YES, -AND I'M ALSO VERY GOOD WITH...

UM...

YOU GOT THE JOB? —OH ASHELLE! I'M SO HAPPY FOR YOU!

GEORGE SAID I WAS *BUBBLY* AND *FRIENDLY* AND THAT THE GUESTS WOULD LIKE THAT.

—BUT HE SAID I WOULD HAVE TO BE A QUICK STUDY.

—THERE ARE A LOT OF THINGS TO LEARN, BUT I'M GOOD AT LEARNING THINGS, SO HE'S GIVING ME A CHANCE.

I'M SO EXCITED!

WHEN DO YOU START?

ON TUESDAY.

—BUT GEORGE IS GOING TO START TRAINING ME TOMORROW.

THERE ARE A LOT OF THINGS I NEED TO PRACTICE.

—HE'S GOING TO TEACH ME HOW TO USE A VACUUM AND HOW TO PUT THINGS ON TRAYS IN AN ELEGANT WAY, AND HOW TO POUR WINE AND ANSWER THE PHONE IN A RELAXED BUT PROFESSIONAL MANNER.

IT'S GOING TO BE VERY CHALLENGING, BUT I'M GOING TO TRY VERY HARD AND BE THE BEST EMPLOYEE HE'S EVER HAD.

I'VE MADE UP MY MIND!

WOW. YOU'RE VERY INSPIRING TO LISTEN TO WHEN YOU'RE EXCITED ABOUT SOMETHING.

SO, HOW DID IT GO WITH MY UNCLE?

SHE GOT THE JOB!

I'M GOING TO BE WORKING HERE!

RIGHT ON!

BUT I NEED TO FIND SOME NICE CLOTHES. —MY JUMPSUIT ISN'T APPROPRIATE FOR A B&B, EVEN IF IT IS MODERN AND FASHIONABLE.

CAN WE TAKE ASHELLE TO THE DISCOUNT CLOTHING STORE?

SURE! WHY NOT?

I WANT TO WEAR BEAUTIFUL PUFFY SKIRTS LIKE THE ONES IN THE PICTURES YOU SHOWED ME.

THOSE WERE WEDDING DRESSES.

YES! LIKE THOSE!

DID YOU WARN YOUR UNCLE LIKE I SAID THAT SHE'S SORT OF DIFFERENT?

AW, WHY ARE YOU WORRYING SO MUCH, TOM? —SHE SEEMS FINE.

YEAH...

WHY AM I WORRYING ABOUT HER SO MUCH..?

CHAPTER SIX

"COMPATIBILITY ISSUES"

LATER THAT WEEK...

WHAT ARE YOU LOOKING AT..?

YOU SEE THAT COUPLE OVER THERE?

THAT TALL GIRL AND THE SHORT GUY?

YEAH! OUT OF ALL THE COUPLES, THEY'RE MY FAVORITE.

YOU HAVE FAVORITE COUPLES?

SURE.

THEY DO SEEM HAPPY.

SHE HAS AN ODD SMILE.
—IT LOOKS SO PRETTY.
THEY'RE SO CUTE!
—THEY HOLD HANDS.

I SEE THEM AROUND TOWN, AND I WATCH THEM.

THEY HAVE A VERY GENTLE AND LIGHT WAY ABOUT THEM.

YEAH. THEY SEEM NICE, I GUESS.

AND I DON'T WANT TO KNOW ANYTHING ABOUT THEM! —NOTHING ABOUT THEIR LIVES.

—I DON'T WANT TO KNOW ANY DETAILS ABOUT THEIR RELATIONSHIP!

I KNOW ALL ABOUT RELATION-SHIPS!
—THEY'RE ALWAYS COMPLICATED.

RELATIONSHIPS ARE TOO MUCH TROUBLE.

COMPLICATED DOESN'T HAVE TO MEAN 'BAD'.

BOOM

WE'RE HERE, MY LADY.

SO... THIS IS ASHELLE'S LITTLE PLANET.

HM...

IT IS RATHER LOVELY. —HER FATHER GAVE HER A FINE WORLD.

I AM SURE SHE WILL SQUANDER ITS ABUNDANCE.

NOW... WHERE HAS THAT GIRL HIDDEN HERSELF..?

—NO DOUBT SHE DIDN'T WALK TEN PACES FROM HER ARRIVAL POINT BEFORE FALLING IN LOVE WITH SOME RUDDY LITTLE HAMLET.

—I EXPECT BY NOW SHE'S WEARING A GRASS HAT AND RAISING CROPS.

—OR A PEASANT ARMY.

HM... —I'VE GOT TO FIND HER.

BRUSILUS, BRING THE LUGGAGE.

YES, MY LADY.

ASHELLE?

I DON'T REALLY KNOW WHAT THE ANSWER IS YET...

BUT I THINK IT HAS TO DO WITH RECOGNIZING THAT NONE OF US LIVES FOREVER, AND THAT WE ARE ALL PART OF A CYCLE.

—THAT'S WHAT TOM WAS SAYING.

TOM..?

THE LAWNCARE PEOPLE WERE KILLING ALL THE DANDELION FLOWERS AT THE B&B, AND MY BOSS TOLD ME THAT THIS WAS NORMAL BEHAVIOR.

I WAS VERY UPSET.

THEN ON MY WAY HOME, TOM GAVE ME SOME FLOWERS.

—I TOOK ONE LOOK AT THEM AND TURNED INTO A BLUBBERING IDIOT. —THEN I YELLED AT HIM.

IT WAS AN UGLY SCENE.

TOM GAVE YOU FLOWERS? WOW!

YES. —HE SAID THEY WERE WILD-FLOWERS.

—THERE WERE SOME DANDELIONS AMONG THEM, WHICH IS WHY I BECAME SO EMOTIONAL.

GOSH!

—SO HE TOLD YOU THAT HE WAS IN LOVE WITH YOU?

—EXCEPT, YOU CAN'T LET UN-AVOIDABLE EMOTION RULE YOUR LIFE.

—YOU HAVE TO COME TO TERMS.

—SO WHAT I'M THINKING IS THAT IF YOU MUST KILL IN ORDER TO LIVE, THEN YOU SHOULD DO IT IN A WAY WHICH IS RESPECTFUL.

—I THINK THAT MIGHT HELP MAKE IT BETTER.

IT'S LIKE AN AGREEMENT BETWEEN YOUR-SELF AND OTHER CREATURES.

TOO MANY THINGS ARE HAPPENING!

—I WAS IN A WAR, AND THEN I WAS UNEMPLOYED.

—AND THEN THE LAWNCARE MILITIA WERE SPRAYING POISON.

AND NOW SOMEBODY IS IN LOVE WITH ME! IT'S TOO MUCH TO HANDLE! I'M ALL FLUSTERED!

—MY FACE IS GETTING HOT!

BANG BANG

ARGH! IT'S TOM!

WHAT DO I DO? I CAN'T TALK TO HIM RIGHT NOW!

I DON'T THINK IT'S HIM.

IT'S HIM! I KNOW IT'S HIM! —TELL HIM TO GO AWAY!

—NO, NO..!

—BUT BE NICE! I DON'T WANT TO UPSET HIM.

OOOOH! THIS IS TOO MUCH!

OH GOD! —HOW COULD THIS GET ANY WORSE?!

JUST ANSWER THE DOOR AND THINK OF SOMETHING GOOD TO SAY —YOU'RE SMART!

GOOD DAY. THE LADY GORVA KYTANNA OF THE GALACTIC IMPERIUM SEEKS THE PRINCESS ASHELLE.

34

ARGH!!

CHAPTER SEVEN

"FRIENDS AND FAMILY"

KYTANNA! WHAT ARE YOU DOING HERE?!

WELL, WHAT WAS *I* SUPPOSED TO DO?

—YOU FLED THE IMPERIUM AND THE MOST **GHASTLY** RUMORS BEGAN CIRCULATING.

—PEOPLE ARE SAYING THAT YOU JOINED THOSE FILTHY **REVOLUTIONARIES!**

OBVIOUSLY I HAD TO COME LOOKING FOR YOU!

THEY'RE NOT FILTHY!

—THEY'RE FIGHTING *TYRANNY* AND *SLAVERY!* —IT'S A *NOBLE* CAUSE!

GASP!

SO IT'S TRUE! —YOU'VE JOINED THE REBELS AND NOW YOU'RE A TRAITOR TO THE EMPIRE!

OH, THE **SHAME!**

WELL... I DIDN'T *JOIN* THEM, EXACTLY... —THEY TOOK ME *HOSTAGE.*

—AND THEY **BRAIN-WASHED** YOU INTO SUPPORTING THEIR CAUSE?

IT'S *NOT* LIKE *THAT* !

WELL WHAT EXACTLY *IS* IT LIKE, THEN?

UM.., WELL..,

ONE THING LED TO ANOTHER AND I SORT OF BECAME THEIR LEADER.

THEIR *LEADER*?!

RRR! IT'S NOT POSSIBLE!

YOU CAN'T BE A MILITARY GENIUS! YOU JUST **CAN'T**!

-YOU'RE A **NIT WIT**! -A **KLUTZ**! **ARGH**!

-YOU'RE WRECKING MY ENTIRE VIEW OF REALITY!

WELL BOO-HOO! WAR IS **INSANE**! WAR IS ALL ABOUT MAKING A BUNCH OF REGULAR PEOPLE DO THINGS NOBODY BUT A **LUNATIC** WOULD WANT TO DO!

-AT LEAST THAT'S HOW THE TROOPS UNDER MY **FATHER'S** COMMAND ARE; -THEY'RE ALL EITHER **CRAZY** OR BEING TRICKED INTO **ACTING** CRAZY.

-IF THE WAR ENDED TOMORROW, HALF OF THEM WOULD STILL BE SOLDIERS.

THAT'S **CRAZY**!

BUT THE PEOPLE I WAS LEADING ARE FIGHTING FOR THEIR **FREEDOM**.

IF THE WAR ENDED TOMORROW, THEY'D ALL GO HOME AND NEVER WANT TO FIGHT AGAIN.

WHY IS IT SUCH A MYSTERY THAT SANE PEOPLE CAN OUT-SMART A BUNCH OF **PSYCHOTICS**?

THAT'S **PHILOSOPHICAL**! -YOU ARE A MILITARY GENIUS! **I CAN'T STAND IT**!

IT'S COMMON SENSE! UGH! -YOU ALWAYS MAKE ME ANGRY WHENEVER YOU SHOW UP. -WHY DID YOU EVEN COME HERE?

BECAUSE I MISSED YOU.

SO, THIS IS WHERE YOU ARE STAYING?

YES...

HOW MODEST. -BUT IF **YOU** CAN MANAGE, I'M SURE I CAN AS WELL.

HOLD ON.

WHAT ARE YOU SAYING, EXACTLY?

-WELL, YOU DIDN'T EXPECT ME TO TRAVEL ALL THIS WAY JUST TO TURN AROUND AND LEAVE AGAIN, DID YOU?

I'M STAYING HERE WITH YOU, OF COURSE!

-I'VE NEVER BEEN ABLE TO DECIDE WHETHER YOUR FONDNESS FOR THE PEASANT LIFE STYLE WAS **CHARMING** OR **INFANTILE**...

HOLD ON!

YOU CAN'T JUST INVITE YOURSELF INTO MY LIFE!

-AND ANYWAY, YOU HAVE TO ASK **JEN** FIRST!

OH, PFT. —I'M SURE YOUR LITTLE FRIEND WON'T MIND ANOTHER GUEST, WILL YOU, DEAR?

UM... WELL ACTUALLY, THERE'S **ANOTHER WHOLE ROOM** WHICH THE LANDLADY IS STILL TRYING TO RENT OUT. —SO IT'S NOT REALLY UP TO ME.

JEN!!

SETTLE DOWN. —I WON'T INTRUDE UPON YOUR AFFAIRS.

YOU'RE ALREADY INTRUDING!

I CAME HERE TO GET AWAY FROM THE EMPIRE, NOT HAVE IT **MOVE IN** WITH ME!

DON'T BE SILLY, DEAR. I'M HARDLY THE EMPIRE.

BRUSILUS, FETCH MY LUGGAGE. —JEN, DEAR, SHOW ME TO THE ROOM, PLEASE.

YES M'LADY.

WELL, IT'S UPSTAIRS...

WHAT SORT OF MEALS WILL YOU BE PREPARING, JEN?

KYTANNA! JEN IS MY **FRIEND**! —SHE'S NOT GOING TO BE YOUR SERVANT!

UGH!

THIS IS HAPPENING TOO QUICKLY! —HOW DOES SHE ALWAYS **DO** THIS TO ME??

YOU'RE NOT MOVING IN HERE KYTANNA!

—I REFUSE TO LET YOU DOMINATE MY LIFE AGAIN!

ONE RELAXING ISLAND GET-AWAY COMING UP!

SO WHAT IS IT?
—SCHOOL GETTING YOU DOWN?

NO.
—I WAS LUCKY ENOUGH TO ESCAPE MY SCHOOL WITHOUT INJURY.

I CAN'T SAY I'VE HEARD IT PUT THAT WAY BEFORE.

IT WAS A DARING BUT NECESSARY ADVENTURE, THOUGH NOW I AM HUNTED.

ONE OF MY OLD CLASS-MATES HAS FOLLOWED ME ACROSS THE GALACTIC WASTES, AND NOW SHE'S MOVING IN WITH ME!

SHE WASN'T INVITED!
—AND MY BEST FRIEND IS CHARMED BY HER!

—AND I JUST KNOW SHE'S GOING TO GET TREATED LIKE THE REST OF KYTANNA'S SERVANTS.

—AND ALSO, THERE'S A BOY WHO HAS FALLEN IN LOVE WITH ME, AND I DON'T EVEN KNOW IF OUR SPECIES ARE COMPATIBLE!

WHOA.
—YOU'RE LOSING ME WITH ALL THE METAPHOR.

THAT'S BECAUSE I'M NOT USING METAPHOR.
—I'M TIRED OF PRETENDING TO BE SOMEBODY I'M NOT!

YEAH, IT CAN BE IF YOU DON'T LEARN TO—

AND I KNOW FROM EXPERIENCE THAT I CAN BE AN OVER-WHELMING PERSON. —BEING FROM A **VAST GALACTIC EMPIRE** MAKES ME A PECULIARITY, BUT I WON'T BOTHER YOU WITH ANY MORE UNREQUESTED DETAILS.

PLEASE FEEL FREE TO FORGET ALL ABOUT IT.

WELL, YOU **ARE** A BIT—

I'M **ASHELLE** BY THE WAY.

WHAT'S YOUR NAME?

OH, PLEASED TO MEET YOU. I'M—

BECAUSE I'M STILL **NEW** HERE AND I'M HOPING TO MAKE FRIENDS WHO ARE **PATIENT** WITH PEOPLE WHO HAVE WEIRD TENDENCIES.

—TO ME, THIS WHOLE PLANET IS **SUPREMELY ODD** AND I'M FINDING IT HARD TO FIGURE IT ALL OUT.

—NOT **ODD** IN A **BAD** WAY, OF COURSE. —THE EARTH IS VERY NICE.

THANKS. I LIKE IT.

YOU KNOW, I CAN'T FIGURE OUT WHY THEY SAY COFFEE SHOPS OFFER "A RELAXING SOCIAL ENVIRONMENT."

—I DON'T FEEL RELAXED AT ALL!

YOU **DO** KNOW THAT CAFFEINE IS A **STIMULANT**, RIGHT?

OOOH!

AND I JUST **LOVE** THE WALL HANGINGS! DID YOU PAINT THEM ALL YOURSELF?

BUMP

PLEASE TELL ME YOU DIDN'T DRIVE HERE.

THE NEXT DAY...

MY LADY! I WAS SUCCESSFUL IN OBTAINING A QUANTITY OF THIS PLANET'S CURRENCY.

EXCELLENT! IS THIS A LOT?

BY MY ESTIMATES, IT SHOULD BE ENOUGH TO SECURE FOOD AND SHELTER FOR HALF AN EARTH STANDARD YEAR.

WAS IT DIFFICULT TO COME BY?

THERE ARE A NUMBER OF AUTOMATIC DISPENSARIES IN THIS SETTLEMENT.

IT WAS A SIMPLE MATTER TO FOOL THE MECHANISM'S SECURITY SYSTEM.

HA! -AND ASHELLE THOUGHT I WAS GOING TO HAVE TO STOOP TO WORKING.

-I CAN'T WAIT TO SEE HER FACE WHEN SHE SEES THIS. HEH! HEH!

HI, EVERYBODY! I'M HOME!

AH! -HELLO, ASHELLE.

HOW WAS YOUR DAY AT WORK?

IT WAS AMAZING!

HI, ASHELLE! GOSH, YOU LOOK HAPPY.

I AM! -MY BOSS STARTED HAVING ME WELCOME THE GUESTS WHEN THEY ARRIVE AT THE B&B, AND I MET THE MOST WONDERFUL COUPLE!

THEIR NAMES ARE JIM AND SARAH, AND WE SAT TOGETHER AND TALKED ABOUT JUST EVERYTHING!

-THEY'VE TRAVELED ALL OVER THE EARTH, AND THEY HAVE SUCH INCREDIBLE STORIES.

THE NEXT DAY...

HRM!

THE LIFE OF AN *IMPERIAL BODYGUARD* IS NOT AN EASY THING.

NERVES OF *ADMANTIUM*, PERFECTION OF *BODY* AND *MIND* ARE ESSENTIAL.

THE IMPERIAL WARRIOR MUST PUT ASIDE ALL PERSONAL NOTIONS.

THERE IS BUT *ONE* PURPOSE IN LIFE...

TO SERVE WITHOUT FAIL OR JUDGEMENT HIS CHARGE!

—IN MY CASE, THE GLORIOUS *LADY KYTANNA!*

I AM EMBARKED UPON A MISSION TO SABOTAGE THE *PRINCESS ASHELLE* IN HER JOYFUL PLACE OF EMPLOYMENT.

TO COVERTLY BRING HER TO *RUIN!*

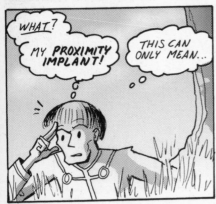

THIS REALLY BURNS ME UP! —YOU'RE OBVIOUSLY A GOOD PERSON.

OUR MASTER WOULD NOT HAVE TRAINED HIM WERE IT NOT SO.

BUT KYTANNA KEEPS MAKING YOU DO EVIL THINGS!

WELL, I WOULDN'T NECESSARILY CALL IT EVIL HER LADYSHIP SIMPLY HAS A PARTICULAR WAY ABOUT HER...

—YOU BLEW UP PRINCESS NATALIA'S PRIVATE SCHOONER. WITH ALL HANDS ABOARD...

THAT WAS YOU?!

ER... THE SHIP WAS SUPPOSED TO BE EMPTY AT THE TIME...

ARGH! AND ALL BECAUSE KYTANNA COULDN'T STAND SOMEBODY ELSE HAVING A NICER SHIP THAN HERS! SEE? THIS IS WHAT I'M TALKING ABOUT!

AND THIS IS BAD FOR YOU, BRUSILLUS!

EVERY TIME YOU DO SOMETHING EVIL, YOU KILL A PIECE OF YOUR SOUL.

BUT... TO DISOBEY... —WITHOUT MY HONOR, WHAT HAVE I?

DUH! —YOUR SOUL?!

BRUSILLUS! I WANT YOU TO FIX THIS! —YOU HAVE TO QUIT WORKING FOR THAT GIRL!

—WELL, ACTUALLY... I'D HAVE TO KILL HIM IF HE DID THAT. —THE IMPERIAL GUARD CORPS IS OBLIGATED TO ENFORCE THESE LAWS.

GRR!! —YOU AND YOUR INSANE HONOR SYSTEM!

THE CODE HAS KEPT THE CORPS RELIABLE FOR A THOUSAND YEARS.

IMPECCABLY SO.

WELL, DON'T **I** HAVE ANY SAY..? —MY FATHER'S PRETTY IMPORTANT THESE DAYS. —COULDN'T I JUST ORDER YOU TO—

IT DOESN'T WORK THAT WAY. THE GUARD-CORPS STANDS OUTSIDE THE AUSPICES OF IMPERIAL LAW.

IT MAKES US EFFECTIVE AND TRUST-WORTHY.

THE ONLY REAL WAY OUT OF KYTANNA'S SERVICE IS TO SACRIFICE MYSELF IN AN **HONORABLE DEATH**...

OH **NO** YOU **DON'T**!

YOU'RE NOT GOING TO DIE BECAUSE **SHE** HAPPENS TO BE A **SELFISH IDIOT**!

THERE'S **GOT** TO BE ANOTHER WAY!

THIS IS NOT A **NEW PROBLEM**, PRINCESS. —IT'S THE LUCK OF THE DRAW. —EVERY DAY I AM THANKFUL TO HAVE BEEN ASSIGNED TO YOUR SERVICE.

IT IS MY PRIVATE HOPE THAT ONE DAY LADY **KYTANNA** WILL SOFTEN IN HER WAYS...

PSH. —NOT MUCH CHANCE OF _THAT_.

LOOK. —FROM NOW ON, ANY TIME SHE GIVES YOU AN ORDER YOU DON'T LIKE, COME TO **ME** AND I'LL **FIX** IT.

MY AUTHORITY GIVES ME **THAT** MUCH POWER, ANYWAY.

YOU GOT THAT?

HMM... IT IS **SNEAKY** AND **DISHONEST**. —THE COUNCIL WOULD NOT APPROVE.

WE COULD BOTH LOSE OUR HEADS OVER IT...

WELL, WHO'S GOING TO KNOW?

...

CHAPTER EIGHT

"REALITY KNOCKS"

A MYSTERIOUS FIGURE DRIVES INTO TOWN...

I HATE FLYING, BUT TWO SOLID DAYS BEHIND THE WHEEL?

UGH!

HM... I DROVE THROUGH SOME SORT OF BOUNDARY...

AND THERE'S TWO CONVERGING ENERGY LINES I CAN SEE JUST FROM HERE.

CLK

THIS WHOLE PLACE MUST KEEP EVERYBODY IN QUITE AN ACCELERATED STATE.

OKAY.

PFF

LET'S GET TO WORK.

WELL NOW! —THE REAL DEAL! CHALK ANOTHER ONE UP FOR THE OLD MAN.

EXCUSE ME, BUT DO YOU MIND IF I SHARE THIS TABLE WITH YOU?

ALL THE OTHERS ARE TAKEN.

NOT AT ALL. —PLEASE.

THANK-YOU!

—I'M ASHELLE, BY THE WAY.

HAVE WE MET BEFORE?

—I JUST DROVE IN TODAY.

FUNNY... I COULD SWEAR...

HOLD ON!

I DO KNOW YOU!!

YOU'RE DANGEROUS!!

ARGH! —DON'T PROVOKE THEM! —YOU HAVE NO IDEA WHAT THEY'RE CAPABLE OF!

YEAH? WELL, THAT WORKS BOTH WAYS!

I DIDN'T COME HERE TO FIGHT, BUT I'M IN A ROTTEN MOOD AND I HAVE COMPLETELY HAD IT WITH ALIEN JERKS!

OH NO YOU DON'T!

YOU'RE ONE OF THOSE MARTIAL ARTS PEOPLE! —YOU PRETEND TO BE ALL CALM AND WISE, BUT REALLY YOU'RE JUST WISHING FOR AN EXCUSE TO SHOW HOW SPECIAL YOU ARE!

WELL, YOU'RE NOT SMASHING UP MY FAVORITE COFFEE SHOP AND MAYBE GETTING PEOPLE HURT JUST TO SATISFY YOUR EGO!

IF THE THREE OF YOU HONESTLY WANT TO KILL EACH OTHER, THEN DO IT OUTSIDE SO THE REST OF US CAN IGNORE YOU!

SO..., THAT'S WHAT YOU ARE. A PROTECTOR.

WHAT? I'M JUST ME!

BUT YOU'RE OBVIOUSLY MORE THAN JUST A REGULAR GIRL!

SO WHY DON'T YOU TELL US WHO **YOU** ARE AND **WHY** YOU CAME HERE?

FAIR ENOUGH. —I CAME TO GET AN IDEA OF WHAT WE'RE INVOLVED WITH.

TO SEE YOU FOR **MYSELF**.

INVOLVED WITH? —I DON'T EVEN **KNOW** YOU!

DON'T BE SILLY! YOU THINK YOU CAN MESS AROUND THE WAY YOU'VE BEEN DOING WITHOUT ANYBODY NOTICING?

THERE HAVE BEEN **BATTLE CRUISERS** IN AND OUT OF ORBIT OVER THIS LOCATION FOR TWO MONTHS NOW!

THERE HAVE BEEN **PENETRATIONS** THROUGH THE REALITY CURTAIN AND **TWO** PHYSICAL LANDINGS!

THESE COORDINATES ARE GLOWING HOT ON A DOZEN COMMAND STATIONS ALL AROUND THE GLOBE!

REALLY..? OH.

—I'D SORT OF HOPED NOBODY WOULD NOTICE.

GET REAL!!

I HAD TO PERSONALLY INTERVENE TO STOP THIS TOWN FROM BEING DESCENDED UPON BY TWO DIFFERENT PARA-MILITARY GROUPS!

—A COUPLE OF ILLUMINATI WIZARD MORONS WERE EVEN PLANNING TO SHOW UP!

THINGS HAVE BEEN HANGING BY A THREAD!

GOSH. I HAD NO IDEA.

WELL I'D CERTAINLY BE ANNOYED IF YOU WERE CAUSING THIS MUCH TROUBLE ON **PURPOSE**!

I DIDN'T REALIZE THE HUMAN POPULATION WAS SO.., _AWARE_.

THERE ARE DIFFERENT LEVELS AT WORK.

SO WHAT I NEED TO KNOW IS, WHAT ARE YOU TRYING TO _ACHIEVE_?

ACHIEVE? I SAID ALREADY. _NOTHING_.

THOUGH... I WAS SORT OF HOPING TO...

YES?

WELL... I WAS THINKING OF STARTING A _VEGETABLE_ GARDEN.

—I WANT TO GET A PIECE OF LAND WHERE PEOPLE COULD PLANT TOMATOES AND SUNFLOWERS AND BEANS.

BEANS?

AND THEN AT THE END OF THE YEAR WE COULD ALL HAVE A BIG PARTY WHERE WE MAKE DISHES FROM ALL THE THINGS WE GREW. —IT WOULD BE SO MUCH FUN!

THE PRINCESS IS UNIQUE. —IT TAKES A MIND OF _REFINEMENT_ TO UNDERSTAND HER.

—YOUR CONFUSION IS TO BE EXPECTED.

UM.., I THINK HE WAS JUST RUDE TO YOU. SORRY.

OY.

JUST WHEN I THINK THIS JOB CAN'T GET ANY _MORE_ WEIRD...

SO LET ME GET THIS STRAIGHT... —YOU'RE TELLING ME THAT YOU HAVE **NO** MISSION PROFILE WHATSOEVER?

—NOBODY SENT YOU HERE TO DELIBERATELY AFFECT HUMAN CULTURE?

NO.

I RAN AWAY.

HM... WELL, I CAN'T SEE ANY BAD STRINGS ATTACHED WHEN I LOOK AT YOU...

STRINGS?

YOUR ENERGY IS CLEAN.

MY WHAT?

YOU WILL DETECT NO CORRUPTIONS WITHIN HER.

—THE PRINCESS IS **NOBLE** AND **PURE.**

HMPH. SHE'S A **TROUBLE-MAGNET,** IS WHAT, SHE IS!

SIGH

WELL... LOOK, I'VE GOT SOME RESOURCES.

—I CAN KEEP THE NASTIES OFF YOUR BACK SO LONG AS YOU DON'T TRY TO DO ANYTHING TOO BIG.

IS MY PUBLIC **VEGETABLE GARDEN** IDEA TOO BIG?

BIGGER THAN YOU THINK, BUT YOUR ENEMIES AREN'T CAPABLE OF RECOGNIZING WHY.

YOU SHOULD BE FINE FOR THE TIME BEING.

BUT YOU DO NEED TO BE CAREFUL...

CAREFUL HOW?

HAVE THERE BEEN ANY **INSERTIONS** LATELY?

ANY HALF-WITTING ATTEMPTS TO **SABOTAGE** YOUR METHODS?

AH! ASHELLE! —THERE YOU ARE!

WE NEED TO HAVE A LITTLE **TALK**.

HELLO, KYTANNA.

I'VE DECIDED IT'S NOT **FAIR** THAT I SHOULD BE EXPECTED TO HELP **CLEAN** THE HOUSE.

WHY?

WELL, YOU'VE BEEN **TRAINED** AT CLEANING AT YOUR JOB. YOU COULD DO THE WORK IN HALF THE TIME, SO IT'S VERY **SELFISH** OF YOU TO DEMAND...

UM...

WHAT'S GOING ON HERE?

LADY KYTANNA, I PRESUME?

WHAT? YES.

I SEE I AM RECOGNIZED BY A **LOWLY** HUMAN.

HOW CHARMING!

—YOU MUST BE OF SUPERIOR STOCK.

SHE FOLLOWED ME TO EARTH AND NOW SHE WON'T GO AWAY.

WAITER!

BRING ME YOUR MOST EXPENSIVE BEVERAGE.

YES MA'AM.

≷SIGH≷ ALL I WANT IS FOR LIFE TO BE A **HAPPY** PLACE.

ME TOO. IT'S HARDER THAN YOU THINK.

CHAPTER NINE

"THE DEEP"

SO WHERE ARE YOU GOING TO GO NOW?

I DON'T KNOW.

THERE'S A LOT TO DO.

THERE'S BEEN FIGHTING IN THE CAUCASUS...

-THE CONTROLLERS ARE MANEUVERING FOR A RENEWAL OF THE COLD WAR.

UM... IS THAT THE ONE WHERE THE SPIES WERE ALL LOOKING FOR MICROFILM?

IT'S JUST MORE STAGING TO BRING MASS PERCEPTION UNDER FINER CONTROL, BUT THAT DOESN'T MAKE IT ANY LESS ANNOYING. -OR DANGEROUS.

I HAD TO CHOOSE WHETHER TO INTERFERE IN THAT OR COME HERE TO MEET YOU.

REALLY? AND YOU CHOSE ME?

SIGH.

-AND LATELY..., I'VE BEEN TEMPTED TO HAVE SOME ARMED DISCUSSIONS WITH THE MEDIA HERE IN THE WEST...

BUT WEEDING THAT GARDEN IS A HUGE JOB, AND I'D PROBABLY GET MYSELF KILLED IN THE PROCESS...

ANYWAY, IT WOULDN'T ADDRESS THE REAL PROBLEM. -YOU CAN'T FIGHT FEAR WITH FEAR...

-IT'S JUST I'VE BEEN SO ANGRY LATELY.

I DON'T FEEL LIKE I'M MAKING ANY DIFFERENCE AT ALL SOME DAYS...

YOU DO SEEM SORT OF UNHAPPY.

MY LIFE IS TOO COMPLICATED.

NOBODY UNDERSTANDS WHAT I'M EVEN TALKING ABOUT HALF THE TIME.

I UNDERSTAND YOU. -I JUST DON'T KNOW ALL THE WORDS YOU'RE USING.

UGH. UNIVERSITIES.

I CAN'T STAND THESE PLACES — I THINK I'D RATHER WAIT OUTSIDE.

NO.

YOU'LL JUST GET COLD TOES AND RUN AWAY.

RUN AWAY?

WHAT MAKES YOU SAY THAT?

JEN'S UP THIS WAY SOMEWHERE.

HEY!

THIS SCHOOL IS ACTUALLY LOTS OF DIFFERENT BUILDINGS. —IT'S SPREAD OUT LIKE A *LITTLE VILLAGE*.

EACH BUILDING IS FULL OF A WHOLE DIFFERENT SUBJECT.

JEN WAS THE FIRST FRIEND I MADE WHEN I CAME TO EARTH.

—SHE LET ME SLEEP ON HER COUCH WHEN I WAS **HOMELESS**,

—SHE'S SUPPORTIVE AND KIND AND SHE IS VERY PATIENT WITH ME, WHICH IS NOT ALWAYS EASY.

WHENEVER I THINK OF HOW KIND SHE WAS WHEN I DIDN'T HAVE ANYBODY, I FEEL ALL TREMBLY INSIDE AND IT MAKES ME WANT TO CRY.

—BUT IN A **GOOD** WAY.

SHE'S THE BEST FRIEND I'VE EVER HAD

I LOVE HER!

OH, ASHELLE..!

PHOO...

OKAY.

—AND THIS IS **NEW** JEN.

SHE'S A VERY POWERFUL **MARTIAL ARTIST.** —SHE KNOWS ALL ABOUT **ALIENS** AND **SECRET THINGS,** AND SHE TRAVELS ALL OVER THE WORLD FIGHTING **TYRANNY!**

GOSH.

I GUESS THAT EXPLAINS THE **NINJA SWORD.**

—WELL, I DON'T **ALWAYS** CARRY IT. BUT THIS TOWN IS CHARGED WITH SOME POWERFUL **CHAOTIC POTENTIALS.**

FOR SOME REASON THOUGH..., —IT SEEMS TO BE **STABLE.**

WOW. —THAT ACTUALLY DESCRIBES THIS PLACE ALMOST EXACTLY.

NEW JEN IS VERY MYSTERIOUS BUT SHE'S SHY ABOUT US ALL GOING TO THE *BEACH* TOGETHER.

—WHICH IS UNDERSTANDABLE.

—SHE'S BEEN CAUGHT UP FOR A LONG TIME IN *PERILOUS* ADVENTURES OF FAR-REACHING IMPORTANCE.

—SHE HAS FORGOTTEN HOW TO CONNECT WITH THE VERY PEOPLE SHE STRIVES TO PROTECT.

A LOST SOUL FILLED WITH BITTER-SWEET REGRETS BUT A STRONG SENSE OF *DUTY,*

—HER EYES BETRAY A *WISDOM* FAR BEYOND HER YEARS.

OKAY... — PLEASE DON'T DO THAT EVER AGAIN.

COME ON! —YOU HAVE TO MEET TOM!

DID SHE SAY WE'RE GOING TO THE BEACH?

SO... ASHELLE SAID SHE COULDN'T INTRODUCE US OR YOU'D GET ANGRY..?

SIGH. YEAH. THAT WAS ME. I NEED TO BE MORE PATIENT.

SHE WAS JUST BEING ENTHUSIASTIC.

HOW LONG HAVE YOU KNOWN HER?

A COUPLE OF YEARS, ON AND OFF.

-BUT I ONLY MET HER TODAY IN PERSON.

REALLY?

-SO YOU MET HER OVER THE INTERNET OR SOMETHING?

HEH.

YEAH. SOMETHING.

I'M STILL SURPRISED SHE WAS ABLE TO REMEMBER.

YEAH! -SHE FOCUSES ON SO MANY DIFFERENT THINGS ALL AT THE SAME TIME. -HER MIND IS AMAZING THAT WAY!

HER MIND IS A MAZE, ALRIGHT.

-EVEN AFTER I FIGURED OUT WHAT WAS GOING ON, IT WAS STILL HARD, WITH HER BEING FROM SO FAR AWAY...

OH! -SO DO YOU KNOW WHERE SHE'S ACTUALLY FROM, THEN?

SHE'S HARDLY PRIVATE ABOUT IT, TOM.

HOPELESSLY IN LOVE.

ALL FLUSTERED.

UM... SO, HOW'S IT GOING?

OKAY, I GUESS.

ACTUALLY, THE TRUTH IS—

—UH!

—YEAH, SO I'M *REALLY* EXCITED ABOUT GOING TO HAVE *ICE CREAM!*

I DON'T KNOW IF I WANT TO TRY **CHOCOLATE** OR *VANILLA*.

I WANT MY FIRST EXPERIENCE TO BE REALLY SPECIAL.

—IF I CHOOSE WRONG, THEN BY THE TIME I FIND THE BEST FLAVOUR, I MIGHT BE TOO **FULL** TO ENJOY IT PROPERLY!

MY MOM HAD THIS OLD *VINYL* COLLECTION.

—THERE WAS A GIRL ON SOME OF THEM WHO LOOKED LIKE YOU.

—I MEAN, *EXACTLY* LIKE YOU.

I DIDN'T REMEMBER UNTIL I WAS WATCHING YOU JUST NOW.

—WHEN I WAS SMALL, I FOUND SOME OF MY MOM'S OLD RECORDS IN THE ATTIC, AND YOUR PICTURE REALLY STRUCK ME.

GOSH.

I DON'T RECALL EVER HAVING BEEN IN A ROCK BAND.

I DON'T KNOW A THING ABOUT MUSIC.

—HER NAME WAS "JENNY MYSTERIOUS."

WHAT?

—WHAT KIND OF DIPPY *STAGE* NAME IS *THAT*?

—IT WAS SORT OF LIKE *STING*, OR *MADONNA*, I THINK.

—80'S STUFF.

I WISH I COULD HAVE LISTENED TO SOME OF THEM, EXCEPT MY MOM'S RECORD PLAYER WASN'T WORKING.

—BUT IT WASN'T YOU, HUH?

THOUGH, SHE EVEN HAD YOUR SAME FIRST NAME! —ISN'T THAT WEIRD? BUT I GUESS IT WAS JUST A COINCIDENCE.

BEH.

—THERE'S NO *'JUST'* ABOUT IT!

—THE ONLY WAY *ANYTHING* HAPPENS IS WHEN FORCES *'CO-INSTANCE.'*

HUMPH!

I KNEW THERE WAS A REASON I WAS NERVOUS ABOUT COMING OUT HERE WITH YOU GUYS.

WHAT A *PAIN!*

HEY, YOU. —YOU LOOK LIKE SOMEBODY WHO IS DEALING WITH MORE THAN SHE BARGAINED FOR.

÷SIGH÷ THAT'S ME.

—I'M NEARING THE END OF A LONG PATH...

—BUT EVEN AFTER EVERYTHING, I STILL HAVEN'T WORKED OUT WHATEVER IT IS I'M SUPPOSED TO DO. —AND I HAVE AN AWFUL FEELING THAT IT'S ALL GOING TO HAPPEN AGAIN.

HA HA!

ALL DREAMS ARE UNIQUE JENNY, BUT YOURS IS SPECIAL.

EXCEPT YOU HAVE BEEN SPENDING MUCH OF IT IN COMPLAINT.

WHO ARE YOU?

REALLY?

YOU HAVE CHOSEN TO FORGET.

THROUGH THIS BODY, UNLESS I BLOCK IT, I FEEL EVERYTHING.

IT ALLOWS ME ACCESS TO MY MEMORIES SOMETIMES. —WHEN IT IS NECESSARY.

BUT WHY?

WHY IS ALL OF THIS HAPPENING TO ME?

—ARE YOUR PEOPLE DOING THIS?

NO. IT'S NOT THEM.

—JENNY, WE EACH WORK IN THE WAYS BEST SUITED.

—EXCEPT YOU HAVE BEEN LIMITING YOURSELF. YOU HAVE TIED A LOT OF KNOTS UP INSIDE. —YOU HAVE ABANDONED YOUR SENSE OF JOY.

JOY?!

HAVE YOU LOOKED AROUND RECENTLY?

—THE WORLD IS BURNING.

CHAPTER TEN

"TREACHERY AND ROMANCE"

SOMETHING HAS TO BE DONE!

I DON'T THINK IT'S ANYBODY'S BUSINESS BUT HERS.

OH, PLEASE! -OF COURSE YOU WOULD BE HAPPY.

IT WOULD PROPEL THIS MISERABLE BACK-END WORLD TO THE CENTER OF THE ROYAL COURT! SPECIAL TREATMENT! -INSTANT AND UN-DESERVING SOCIAL SUCCESS!

ACHT! AND YOUR HIDEOUS CLOTHING!

THOSE PRIMITIVE FASHIONS WOULD BECOME THE NEW VOGUE! -I'D HAVE TO WEAR THAT!

THIS IS A DISASTER! HOW COULD ASHELLE BE SO SELFISH?!

SHE AND I ARE GOING TO HAVE A LITTLE TALK ABOUT THIS!

:AHEM: -MISS JEN, MIGHT I HUMBLY SUGGEST YOU RETIRE TO SOMEWERE.., ER..,

NOT HERE.

NO! ASHELLE NEEDS MY SUPPORT!

NO DOUBT, BUT WITH ALL DUE RESPECT...

-YOU DO NOT COMMAND ANY BATTLE CRUISERS.

WHAT? ARE YOU SERIOUS?!

OH, YES. -COME TO THINK OF IT...

ARE THERE ANY OTHER PLANETS IN THIS SYSTEM WITH BREATHABLE ATMOSPHERES..?

SOOOO...

YES?

DON'T PLAY INNOCENT WITH ME, SISTER!

—I KNOW ALL ABOUT YOU AND THAT *HUMAN MALE!*

TOM?

YES! —JEN TOLD ME ABOUT THE WHOLE SORDID AFFAIR!

SHE DID?

YOU THINK YOU'RE IN LOVE? *BAH!* —YOU'RE SO *IRRESPONSIBLE!*

KYTANNA, **NO.**

JUST FORGET IT.

—I'VE DECIDED THAT YOU'RE NOT GOING TO GET AWAY WITH IT THIS TIME.

WE'RE NOT LITTLE ANYMORE. —I'M STRONG ENOUGH TO NOT BE *CONFUSED* AND *BULLIED* BY YOU.

OH, IS *THAT* WHAT YOU THINK?

IT IS.

AND IF YOU'VE DECIDED TO GET ALL UPSET OVER WHO I CHOOSE TO SPEND MY TIME WITH, THEN THAT'S *YOUR* PROBLEM.

AND IT'S A REAL SHAME!

—OF ALL THE *SELFISH*—

NO. JUST STOP IT.

KYTANNA...

—YOU KEEP *SAYING* YOU'RE MY FRIEND, BUT I DON'T THINK YOU *REALLY* UNDERSTAND WHAT THAT MEANS.

WHAT IS THIS PLACE?

THIS IS THE UNIVERSITY CAMPUS.

PSH.
-SO THIS TOM PERSON IS JUST A STUDENT?

WELL, HE'S PRETTY SMART. -AND HE HAS LOTS OF COOL FRIENDS.

-PEOPLE AROUND HERE LIKE HIM.

UGH.
ASHELLE HAS GALACTIC LORDS INTERESTED IN HER!

IF SHE PLAYS HER CARDS RIGHT, SHE COULD BE QUEEN OF THE ENTIRE IMPERIUM!

WHAT MAKES SOME LOUSEY EARTH STUDENT SO SPECIAL?

YOU KEEP SAYING BAD THINGS ABOUT TOM, BUT YOU'VE NEVER EVEN MET HIM!

OH. PLEASE.

JUST SHOW ME WHERE HE IS.

IT MUST BE A LOT HARDER FOR PEOPLE WHO RESIST FLOWING WITH THINGS.

IT'S PROBABLY WHY YOU SEEM SO UNHAPPY.

UNHAPPY?

BUT I HAVEN'T HAD THIS MUCH FUN IN AGES.

—AND THE WHOLE CONCEPT OF A *PSYCHIC FIELD*..!

THE THINGS THAT IMPLIES ..!

—WHY, IT WOULD MEAN—!

HA HA!

ALL THESE NEW IDEAS ARE JUST SO INCREDIBLE!

—IT'S LIKE THE ENTIRE WORLD HAS EXPLODED INTO A *SUN*, BUT WE'RE ALL STILL HERE, ABLE TO MOVE *THROUGH* IT ALL, —TO *EXPERIENCE* IT..!

KYTANNA,

I JUST HAVE TO SAY, IT'S BEEN *REALLY* GOOD MEETING YOU.

I'M *SO* GLAD YOU DECIDED TO COME HERE WITH ASHELLE.

SHE'S LUCKY TO HAVE SUCH *AMAZING* FRIENDS!

OH.

—YOU THINK SO..?

ABSOLUTELY!

—ANYWAY, I HAVE TO GET GOING.

I HAVE A PAPER DUE.

MY PROFESSOR IS GOING TO THINK I'M NUTS!

BYE, TOM!

SEE YOU GUYS LATER!

IT WAS NICE MEETING YOU, TOO!

WHAT DOES HE MEAN 'I DON'T LOOK HAPPY'?

WHY WOULD HE SAY SOMETHING LIKE THAT?

THE NERVE OF THAT GUY!

I DON'T LIKE HIM AT ALL!

HE SEEMS TO THINK YOU'RE PRETTY SPECIAL.

YEAH...

AND YOU WERE REALLY NICE TO HIM.

I HAVE TO ADMIT, I WASN'T EXPECTING THAT FROM YOU.

I'M FEELING CONFUSED.

WELCOME TO MY LIFE.

WELL, IN CASE YOU'RE WONDERING, IT WAS A VERY CONFUSING EVENING.

I WOULD NOT PRESUME TO WONDER ABOUT YOUR AFFAIRS, MY LADY.

PSH. -YOU MIGHT AS WELL START.

-I'VE GOT NOBODY ELSE TO TALK TO.

-AT LEAST I KNOW I CAN TRUST YOU. -ALL OF MY GIRLFRIENDS ARE SELFISH IDIOTS.

I AM HAPPY TO SERVE IN ANY WAY I AM ABLE.

SEE, THE THING IS, I WENT OUT TO SCARE OFF ASHELLE'S NEW BOYFRIEND.

-I WAS REALLY MAD WITH HIM FOR INTERFERING!

WERE YOU SUCCESSFUL?

NO...

HE'S ACTUALLY KIND OF WONDERFUL.

-ALL THE BEST GUYS FALL IN LOVE WITH ASHELLE.

-SHE DOESN'T EVEN HAVE TO TRY.

-I GUESS EVEN ON THIS PLANET, GUYS STILL GO FOR BLOND BUBBLE-HEADS.

DO I SEEM **UNHAPPY** TO YOU?

UNHAPPY, MY LADY ?

HE SAID I WAS **UNHAPPY**.

-NOW I'M ALL **BOTHERED** BY IT.

I DON'T NORMALLY GET BOTHERED BY THINGS PEOPLE SAY TO ME.

HOW DO YOU COPE ?

A TRUE WARRIOR DOES NOT CONCERN HIMSELF WITH THE APPROVAL OF OTHERS.

I REALLY WISH I HAD SOMEBODY ELSE TO TALK ABOUT THIS WITH.

I REGRET NOT BEING SUITABLE.

YOU NEED YOUR PEERS.

KYTANNA?

CAN I COME IN..?

-I BROUGHT YOU UP SOME DINNER.

ARE YOU OKAY?

-YOU SEEMED REALLY UNHAPPY.

UGH.

-MY LIFE HAS BECOME A SAD **PUNCH-LINE** IN SOMEBODY ELSE'S STORY.

CHAPTER ELEVEN

"CHEMISTRY EXPERIMENTS"

THAT NIGHT...

$$e_\mu(p) = (\partial_\mu)p - A^a_m(x,g)\,\varepsilon_\alpha(g),$$
? ? $a = ?$

AND SO...

I WAS USELESS DURING THE **BLACK-HOLE** CRISIS!

IF I'M GOING TO BE WORTHY OF **ASHELLE,** I NEED TO LEARN YOUR **ALIEN SCIENCE.**

WELL, UNLIKE **HER,** I DIDN'T SKIP ANY OF **MY** CLASSES.

I CAN TEACH YOU IF YOU WANT.

$e = MC^2$ YEAH? **AND..?**

I'D REALLY APPRECIATE IT.

—IT WILL GIVE ME SOMETHING TO **DO** ON THIS PLANET, ANYWAY.

—AFTER SHE BROKE MY **TELE-GATE** UNIT, I'M PRETTY MUCH STUCK HERE.

GEE... ISN'T THERE ANY WAY FOR YOU TO GET HOME?

BAH.

—WHAT DOES "HOME" EVEN MEAN?

I DON'T HAVE **ANYONE.**

—ASHELLE IS MY BEST FRIEND, AND EVEN **SHE** DOESN'T LIKE ME..!

SHE **DOES** SEEM PRETTY ANNOYED WITH YOU...

I CAN'T REALLY BLAME HER.

—THERE'S NOT MUCH ABOUT ME WHICH IS VERY LIKABLE.

WHAT?
—YOU SEEM REALLY **GREAT** TO ME.

—I MEAN, YOU FIXED THE **BLACK HOLE** AND SAVED THE **ENTIRE PLANET!**

YEAH, WELL...

I CAN BE PRETTY MEAN AND **SELFISH** SOMETIMES...

HM... THAT'S **WEIRD**.
—ASHELLE WAS SAYING THE SAME THING ABOUT HERSELF EARLIER.

I THINK YOU BOTH MIGHT BE TOO HARD ON YOUR-SELVES.

YEESH...
—IF YOU KNEW SOME OF THE **THINGS** WE'VE DONE...

IT'S JUST SOMEHOW EVERYBODY STILL **LIKES** ASHELLE AFTER SHE PULLS **HER** CRAZY STUNTS.

⇒SIGH⇐

IF I WANT TO HAVE ANY FRIENDS, THEN I NEED TO BE A LOT MORE THOUGHTFUL.

IT'S **HARD**.
—I GET REALLY IMPATIENT AND **SUPERIOR-FEELING** SOMETIMES.

WE ALL HAVE **CHALLENGES**.
—THE IMPORTANT THING IS WHETHER OR NOT WE CHOOSE TO ACCEPT THEM.

—YOU'VE OBVIOUSLY REACHED SOME KIND OF **CRITICAL JUNCTURE** IN YOUR LIFE.

—IT'S INTERESTING THAT YOU CAME HALFWAY ACROSS THE GALAXY TO FIND IT.

—MAKES THE **EARTH** SEEM KIND OF **SPECIAL**, DOESN'T IT?

CHAPTER TWLEVE

"THEN, ALL TOO ABRUPTLY. . ."

BUT... ...

WAIT.., YOU HAVE A *WEDDING* DRESS..?

SHE FOUND IT AT THE DISCOUNT CLOTHING STORE AND WOULDN'T GO HOME WITHOUT IT.

I NEVER GOT A CHANCE TO WEAR IT. —BUT YOU CAN'T HAVE EVERYTHING IN LIFE...

BUT WHAT ABOUT _US_?

WE JUST GOT TOGETHER.

—CAN I COME WITH YOU?

SORRY, TOM. —YOU ARE *DEAR* TO ME, AND WE DIDN'T HAVE LONG THIS TIME, BUT YOU NEED TO STAY BEHIND.

THIS IS JUST FOR ME.

BESIDES, KYTANNA IS THE ONE YOU'RE SUPPOSED TO BE WITH. —AND YOU'RE BOTH FALLING IN LOVE, SO IT ALL WORKS OUT.

WHAT?!

OKAY, EVERYBODY, FOLLOW ME.

THIS NEXT PART IS IMPORTANT.

EPILOGUE

"EVER AFTER"

ASHELLE'S FRIENDS WALKED AWAY. --THEY DIDN'T SPEAK AND THEY DID NOT MAKE EYE CONTACT. NOBODY REALLY KNOWS HOW TO BEHAVE WHEN A BIG GOODBYE HAS COME AND GONE. THE COMFORTABLE PATTERNS OF LIFE COME TO SO MANY ABRUPT HALTS AT, "GOODBYE". FOR JUST A MOMENT, WE WAKE TO REALIZE THAT OUR SCRIPTS HAVE BEEN PULLED AWAY, LEAVING US AIMLESS UPON THE STAGE. THIS IS THE **REAL** US, WHEN THE PAGES OF THE PLAY ARE BLANK WE ARE NO LONGER ABLE TO ACT, WE HAVE ONLY OURSELVES. IT IS BEST TO FIND YOURSELF AT SUCH TIMES WITH PEOPLE WHO REALLY LOVE YOU AND WHO YOU REALLY LOVE. THEY ARE THE ONES WHO WILL FORGIVE YOU EVERY AWKWARD STEP WHEN THE STAGE IS DARK AND THE CROWD MURMURS AND GOD'S EYES ARE UPON YOU. . .

WHAT DO YOU THINK? --IS THAT TOO **MELANCHOLY**? --SHOULD I DO SOMETHING DIFFERENT?

ME.

YES! YOU SHOULD MAKE ME COME BACK!

I DON'T LIKE THAT I HAD TO LEAVE SO SUDDENLY!

WHY DOES STARDROP HAVE TO END?

IT WAS AN EDITORIAL DECISION - THE STORY WAS GETTING TOO SELF-REFERENTIAL.

THE EDITORS WANTED MARK TO DRAW A FRESH STORY; SOMETHING EASIER TO UNDERSTAND.

SOMETHING READERS CAN JUMP IN AND OUT OF WITHOUT COMMITMENT.

SOMETHING SHORTER.

LAST WORDS. . .

It's not really the end!

Well, it nearly was. Let me explain. . .

Stardrop in its original form, runs in a little community paper called, *the Grapevine"*. –The community is Wolfville, where I live, and the managing editors of that little paper are thoroughly decent people (who I must say, put up with my cheek in that last chapter with grace and aplomb. They get high marks just for that.). *Stardrop* is still being produced and will have passed it's 100th episode by the time this book finds its way into comic shops.

But yes, *Stardrop* almost really did get canceled. I'd been drawing comics for the paper now for five or six years since its inception, and I've seen *the Grapevine* move through three different sets of owner/editors, all of whom have brought different strengths to the on-going and much loved little paper. The latest pair to take the helm are very energetic and bright. They breezed in and did something very smart. Determined to shake things up with fresh energy, they ran a poll asking people to rate the various features offered by the paper. They wanted to know what elements should stay and which could do with a trimming. (They also added more pages and several cool new features.)

Now, polls and surveys have become their own industry and there's a reason for that. It takes a lot of work to collect, sort and make sense of social information. Many of you, I suspect at some time have been asked to fill out a questionnaire or spend ten minutes of your valuable time answering a telephone survey. I know I have and I don't usually like it. Thus, out of the couple thousand people who read *the Grapevine,* less than sixty surveys were returned. Among that number, *Stardrop* received lackluster approval. The new editors were understandably concerned. This was a bit sad for me, but it's also the way of the world, so I sighed and thought, "Well, fair enough. Ashelle has had a decent run. Maybe it's time for something new." I asked if I could have the space to run just three more episodes in order to wrap up the story. I was granted this, and so I rolled up my sleeves to get to on with it.

Now, it has been jokingly noted that there are three kinds of lies. "Lies. Damned lies, and *Statistics!"*

Apparently, people who read comics are not the sort of people who fill out polls. As the final episodes of *Stardrop* began pressing, I found myself stopped in the street to answer for my actions. "What's going on!?" "Is *Stardrop* ending?" "What on Earth for?" "But I love *Stardrop!"*

Word on the street soon reached the ears of the editors and the decision to end *Stardrop* was soon reversed. This turn of events was certainly a very happy one for me. Indeed, everybody got something out of the process. A shake-up. A freshening of things! Heck, this print edition exists largely because I (all too abruptly) found myself needing to tie the story down at a nice point where things could be easily broken off, packaged up with a cover and made available in proper book form. It has also shaken things up in the writing department. *Stardrop* has found itself invested with new energies, been sent off in new directions. Sometimes, until threatened with extinction, we simply don't realize how valuable a thing is to us. The universe comes along periodically and forces us to discard that which we no longer need, and to embrace that which is really important. To clean house. We are forced to *choose*.

Well, the choice has been made and I hope to see you all in the next volume!

Cheers, and I wish you all the very best of days!

Mark Oakley
Wolfville, Nova Scotia
April, 2010

The End